BILL WAISER

GORDIE'S SKATE

ILLUSTRATED BY

LEANNE FRANSON

Thistledown Press

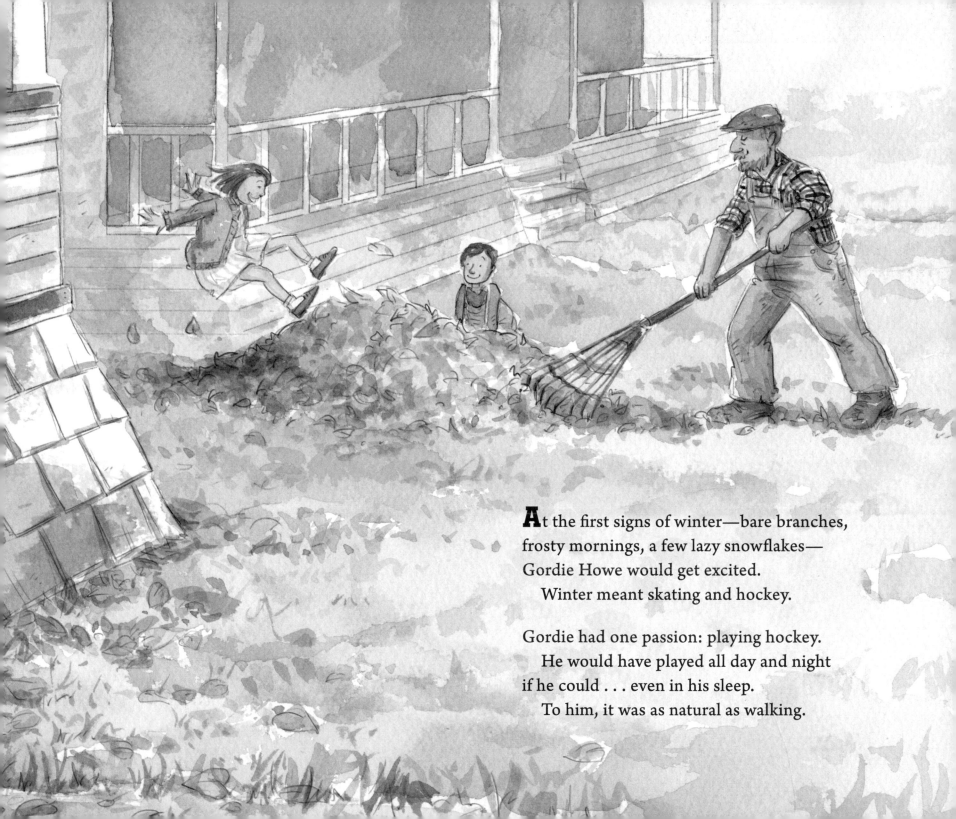

At the first signs of winter—bare branches, frosty mornings, a few lazy snowflakes— Gordie Howe would get excited.

Winter meant skating and hockey.

Gordie had one passion: playing hockey.

He would have played all day and night if he could . . . even in his sleep.

To him, it was as natural as walking.

Gordie was born in 1928 in the tiny village of Floral, Saskatchewan.

The family soon moved to Saskatoon where Gordie's father found a job.

They were lucky. The 1930s were called the Great Depression.

Lots of people couldn't find work.

But even so, the family struggled to make ends meet.

Sometimes Gordie had to eat oatmeal for lunch or supper.

And the house was cold and drafty.

There was also no running water—no taps or drains.

Heavy buckets had to be carried for cooking or washing.

Gordie never complained—but he was often sick.

Gordie's love of hockey began by chance when he was five.

One winter night, a neighbour knocked at the door.

Her husband was sick.

She was desperate.

She told Mrs. Howe she needed money and wanted to sell a sack filled with some of her family's belongings.

Gordie's mother didn't have much money, but she wanted to help.

She handed the woman a bit of change to buy the sack.

She didn't even ask what was inside.

Gordie and his older sister Edna anxiously watched as Mrs. Howe turned the sack upside down and dumped what was inside onto the kitchen floor.

Out tumbled an old pair of men's skates.
SKATES!
Edna took one.
Gordie grabbed the other.

Gordie tried the skate on one foot.
It was way too big.
It was just as big on his other foot.
Gordie stuffed old rags into the skate to make it fit better.
Edna did the same.

Gordie and Edna tried skating by carefully balancing on one foot.

They would push off and wobble across the ice. They didn't get very far and they often fell.

They also tried holding hands and skating together to see if that was better.
    It wasn't.

Even playing hockey was difficult wearing just one skate.

Gordie hustled to keep up with the other players.

He was always left behind, slipping and sliding on the ice.

Edna quickly grew tired of
having only one skate and
left it outside.
    Gordie snatched it.

Now that he had his own pair of skates, Gordie skated everywhere.

He even used the icy ruts in the snow-covered streets of Saskatoon.

Gordie spent hours practicing his shooting.
   His stick blade was worn so thin, it looked
like a giant toothpick!

Over and over, he would snap a tennis ball
against the side of the house, pretending
he was scoring with each shot.
   His father had to nail up a sheet
of plywood to cover the holes.

Gordie never wanted to take his skates off—even in the house!

His mother put newspapers down across the floor so that he could eat his meals with his skates on.

Gordie's favourite place to skate was the frozen Hudson Bay slough.

It stretched for miles, from the back of his house to the Saskatoon airport.

He would skate for hours with his stick and puck, working on his moves, dreaming of playing in the National Hockey League.